Topolino

MAKE-UP GAMES

For Lionel, always there...

© 2001 Assouline Publishing for the present edition
601 West 26th Street, 18th floor
New York, NY 10001
USA
Tel.: 212 989-6810   Fax: 212 647-0005
www.assouline.com

First published by Editions Assouline, Paris, France

Translated from the French by Sandra Petch

Color separation: Gravor (Switzerland)
Printed by Grafiche Milani (Italy)

ISBN: 2 84323 371 2

Topolino

MAKE-UP GAMES

ASSOULINE

Topolino with Zazie, by Jean-Baptiste Mondino. Paris, 2001.

Childhood versus Stereotypes

Each decade has its fashions, its idiosyncrasies, its rituals. Since the flappers took to the streets in visible make-up, the face has become a medium for and an object of fashion. Each era has elected its beauty ideal, invented products and defined appropriate gestures: how to give curve to the eyebrow, fullness to the lips, or just the right length to the lashes. The press catches on to these trends, after which fashions are born and stereotypes created. The story of Topolino couldn't be more different, far from the conventions of make-up, its practices and its preformatted beauties.

Topolino began his career aged nineteen, in *20 Ans* magazine, back in the 1980s. This was a boom time for fashion, a time for showing off, for cheap and chic, for mixing and matching cultures and eras without distinction. Topolino was fresh from Marseilles and an apprenticeship at *L'Atelier Parallèle*, where he had mastered the basics of his trade: hairstyling, fashion, make-up, manicure, etc. Not once did he give in to the prevailing post-modern atmosphere. His work was intentionally free from historical reference or parody. His only inspirations were of his own creation, the fruit of his imagination. Topolino lives in a childhood world, such an endless source of creativity that his first *œil-fleur* ("flower eye"), photographed by Satoshi almost twenty years ago, could have bloomed this very morning.

t opolino, "Mickey Mouse" in Italian, thrives on fantasy, fairy tales and legends. His companions are elves and trolls. He adores clowns as much as cartoons. His sketches have retained all the spontaneity and innocence of his boyhood years. In the blasé world of fashion, Topolino is an exception, unconcerned by the "need" to go one better than the next. He is unique. He is also in demand, leading him to work with Jean-Baptiste Mondino, Jean-Paul Goude, Mario Testino, Annie Leibovitz and Norbert Schoerner, with Pierre et Gilles, Annett Aurell and, from the early years, Bettina Rheims. He creates make-up for photos, music videos and advertisements. He creates make-up for catwalk shows. He creates make-up exactly as he sculpts: for pleasure. Topolino is everywhere. Magazines such as *Glamour, The Face, Femme, Arena, Interview, ID, Vogue, Vogue Homme International, L'Officiel, W, Citizen K, Femme, Jalouse, Jill, Delicia Vitae,* and more are seduced by his world. Barely off the train in Paris, as if by magic the boy from Marseilles became a citizen of the world. Still, even when fame smiles on him, even when his work is shown in museums, Topolino stays true to himself, with his head in the clouds and still signing his sketches with a tiny star.

His style never fails to surprise. He swims against the tide of preconceived ideas, bypasses convention and flirts with subversion.

The skin is his canvas, that of the face and the body, future emblem of the nineties. There is no limit to his inventiveness—a sticking-plaster print, some other home-made beauty accessory, a fake tear in the corner of Björk's eye, pointy ears, a clown's red nose, or razor-sharp glittery Cruella nails. His talent lies in his use of modest means: prisoners' tattoos become an ephemeral decoration that he draws directly on the skin with a ballpoint pen, while a single line across the lips brings the seedy world of junkies onto the pages of the glossiest fashion magazine. Topolino is the master of transformation, the champion of the bizarre, the king of paradox, the virtuoso of subtlety. With humour he brings to light issues that go beyond the framework of fashion. By using fake tan to draw a bikini on a male torso, for example, he suggests the ambiguous nature of sexuality today.

nineties fashion is marked by a certain atonalism: grunge, then minimalist, then internationally chic, grey, black and uniform until one creation blends into another and the "clothes equals fashion" equation loses all meaning. Fashion is elsewhere, in a person's attitude, in the way they move, or wear their hair and make-up. Out on the streets, women are made-up, or not made-up, or made-up but pretending not to be. Meanwhile, piercings, brandings and real tattoos are exposed, ambivalent signs of a desire for freedom and for belonging to a group. Catwalk supermodels are transformed from one show to the next by increasingly extravagant make-up . . . fleeting, yes, but oh! so photogenic beauty. In a word, make-up is all. As always, Topolino revels in excess, finding endless pretexts for amusement, light-heartedly transforming a cow into a gorgeous blonde.

True to his childlike personality, the artist (a status which, out of modesty, he does not proclaim) knows when to abandon surrealist excess to concentrate on the quest for beauty. In his search for the essential, art gives him wings. Lucio Fontana inspires him with the purity of scarification, while Yves Klein brings the magical opposition of blue and gold. Ultimately, however, he captures the very essence of make-up in his own way, brushing a trace of fuchsia pigments across a black cheek, thus capturing in a single gesture the ancestral art of make-up, a combination of ritual body painting, artwork and the quintessence of fashion. Topolino proves that the body, freed from its dependency on clothes and preconceived ideas, is one of the final frontiers of liberty and creativity.

Catherine Ormen

You came into my life thanks to a stuffed monkey. Almost twenty years ago, when you were just starting out, you lavished the savings you didn't have to buy one of my first photos at auction. And so we met. I was touched by your grace. Little did I know just how essential our encounter would be for me.

You are a magician. You don't just make-up women, you illuminate their beauty. Your master José-Luis would tell them, "Darling, you're fresh as a lettuce!" And what do you tell them, Topolino?

You inscribe their skin like a calligrapher, you draw, you imprint, you leave your hallmark on each image taken by the rare few photographers who have the privilege of working with you. There is a Topolino style; your work is unique.

You have been with me in all my madcap adventures, from women who weren't stars to the anonymous faces that were. You even took the risk of turning down work for six months so you could invent the milky skin of virgins and the dying flesh of Christ. You came with us from the shady districts of Paris to Majorca to Los Angeles and other less auspicious places.

Thank you for everything, Topolino. Without you, my work would not have been the same, nor would my life. I forgot to tell you the most important thing of all: you are my friend, and I love you.

Bettina Rheims

i n the beginning. It was a beautiful day. You were sticking
butterflies on her face. Delicately. Concentrated. Precise.
Our first image. Cat. For me, this was where it all began.
One project came after another. Our ideas combined. Friendship,
with its laughter and tears. I learned to know you a little more.

Amused, offbeat, sometimes bitter, you were always in touch with
reality. This is where your genius lies. Absorb, recycle, twist and
deform to recreate "your reality" of childhood, of life and sometimes of death.

You have always chosen the photographers with whom you want to
work. I'm lucky enough to be one of them. Your desire to share
and discover guides you. You couldn't care less about "career"
and "fashion." You are Topolino.

I love your portrait in Marrakech. A shadow on the wall. Peter
Pan never found you. I think you've stopped looking for him too.
You don't need him anymore.

This book isn't the end, it's the beginning.

Éric Traoré

topolino is a twentieth-century boy.

A Marseilles boy in Paris.

Topolino isn't a make-up artist but an artist who works with make-up. He works in fashion but his goal is the image.

He likes hats and shoes and people.

He has a reputation. He's an underground rebel.

Who doesn't make compromises. That would be to misjudge him.

Topo stimulates.

Anyone who wants to understand him can take him to the furthest reaches of the night. To find the Image.

Topolino is sincere and genuine.

With weaknesses and qualities. The most beautiful: his loyalty.

He zaps from experience to discovery.

Topolino isn't a star, even if that's how he signs his work.

Like a mirror, he reflects his times.

Topo is the spiritual son of Peter Pan and Mickey Mouse.

Topolino is Jean Cocteau meets Walt Disney!!!

Lionel Bouard

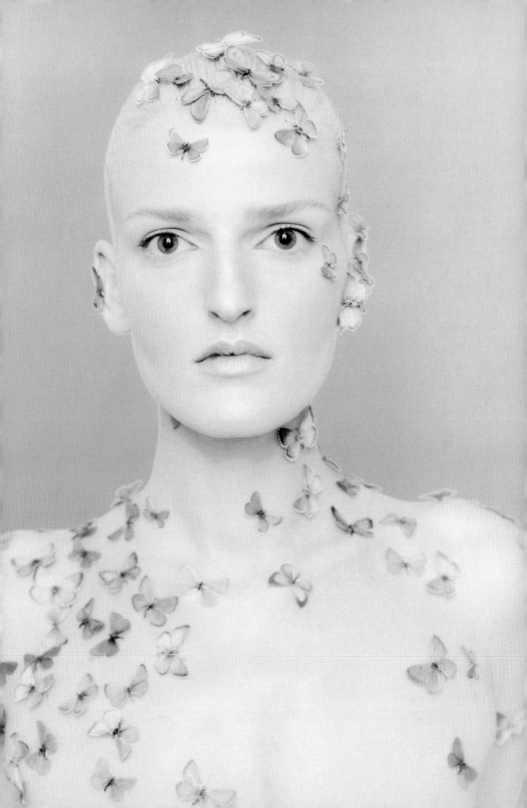

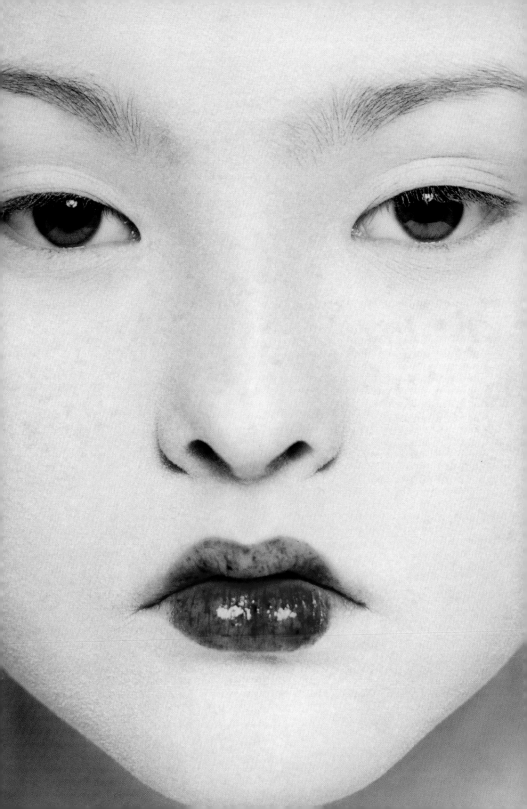

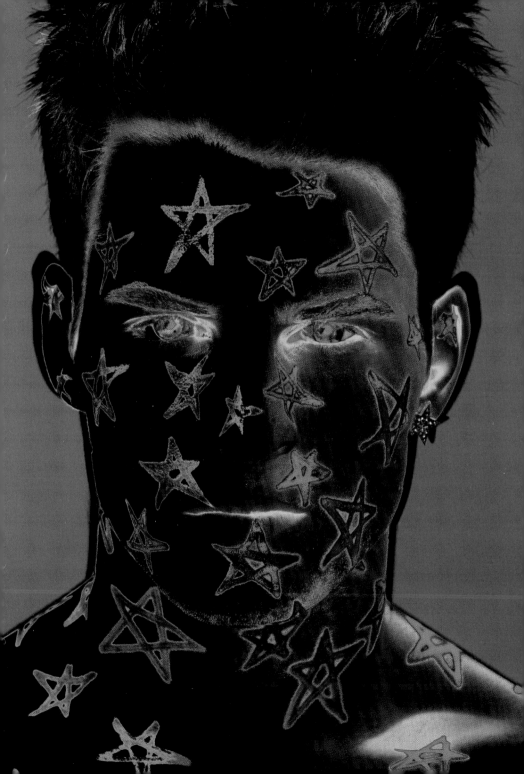

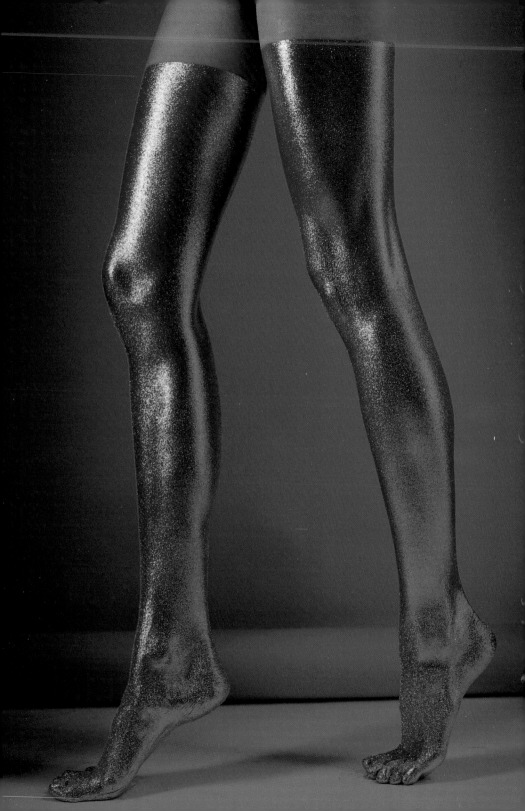

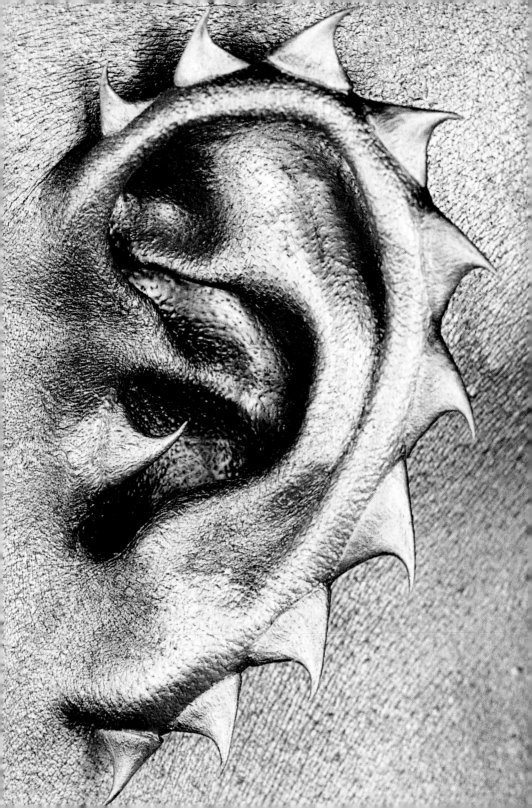

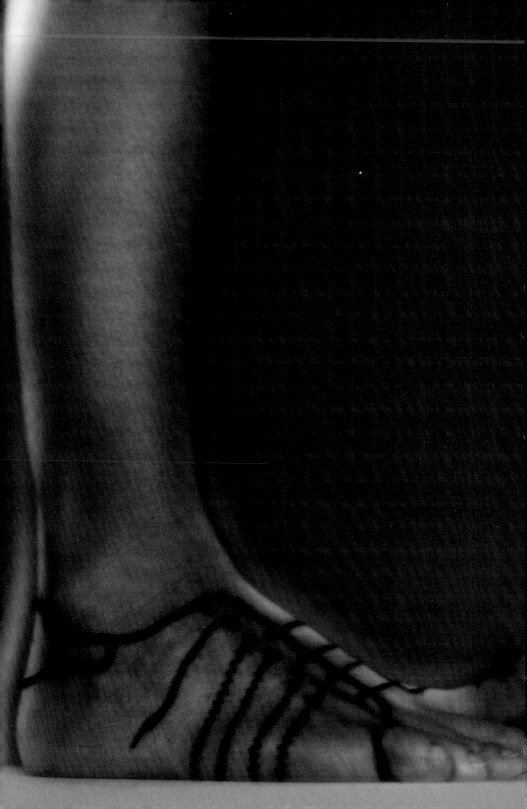

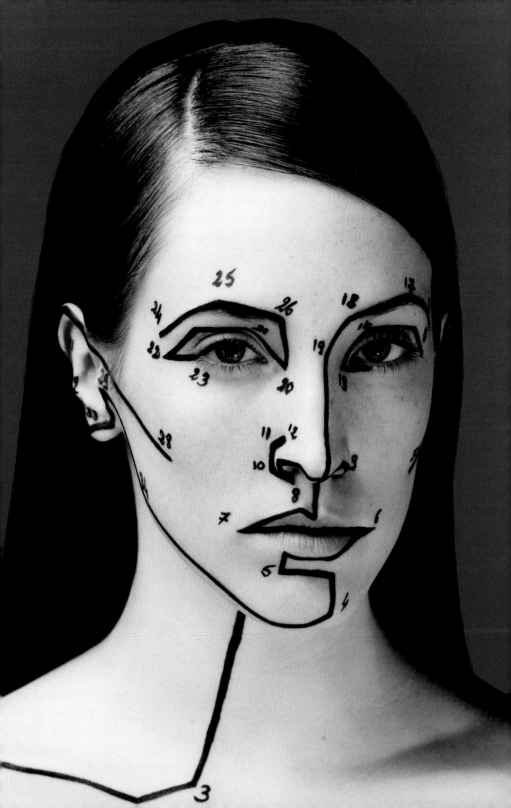

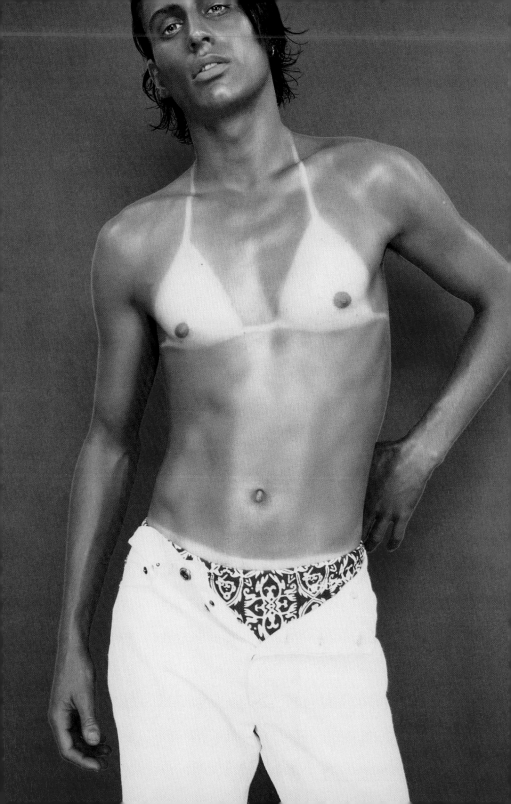

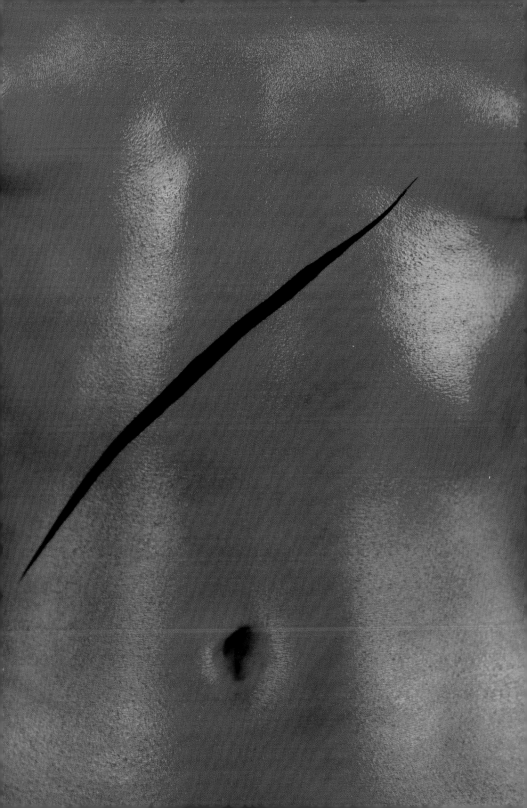

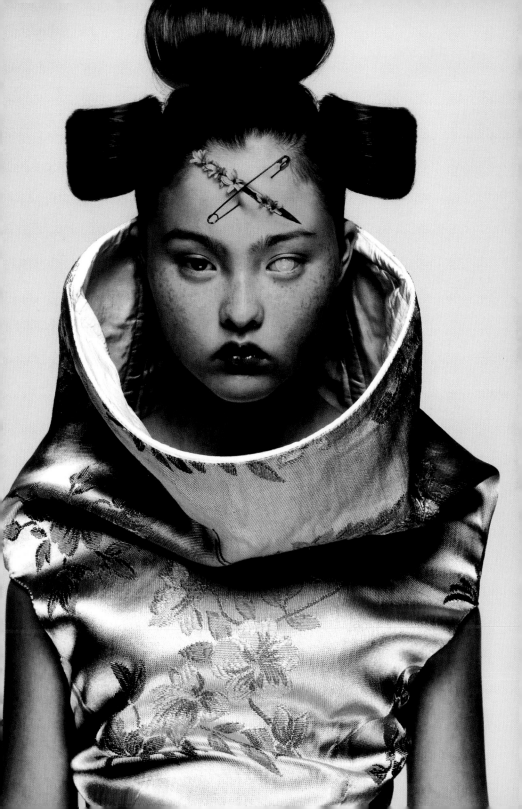

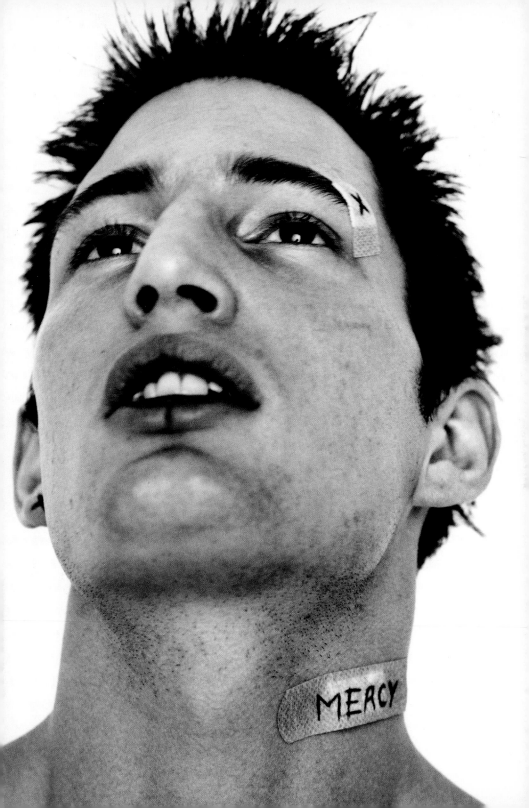

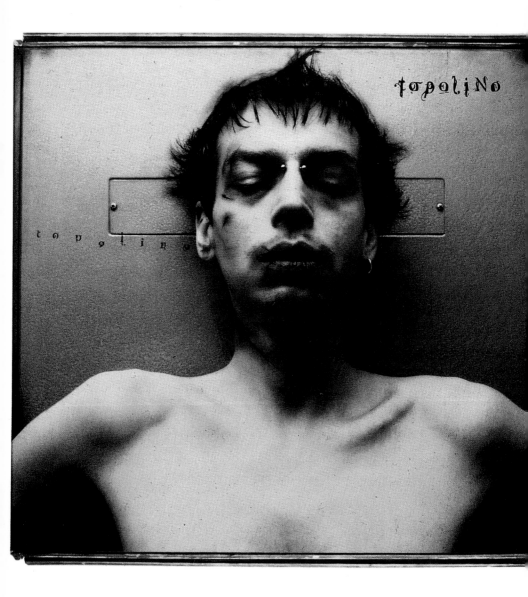

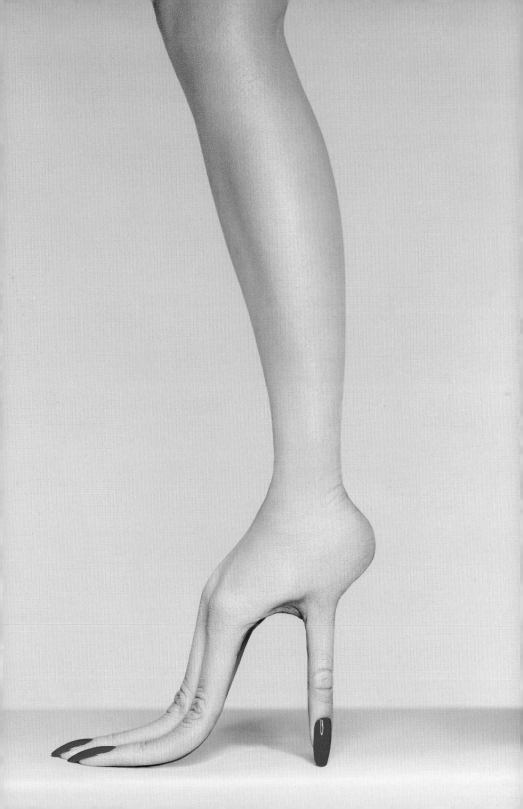

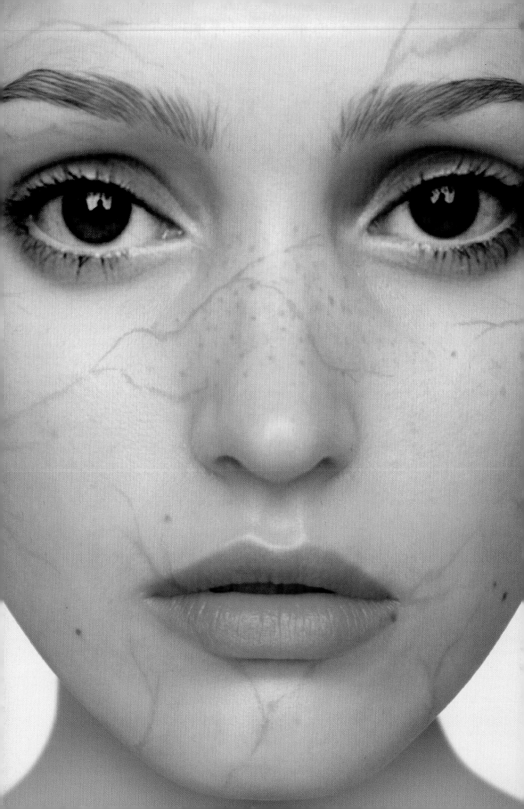

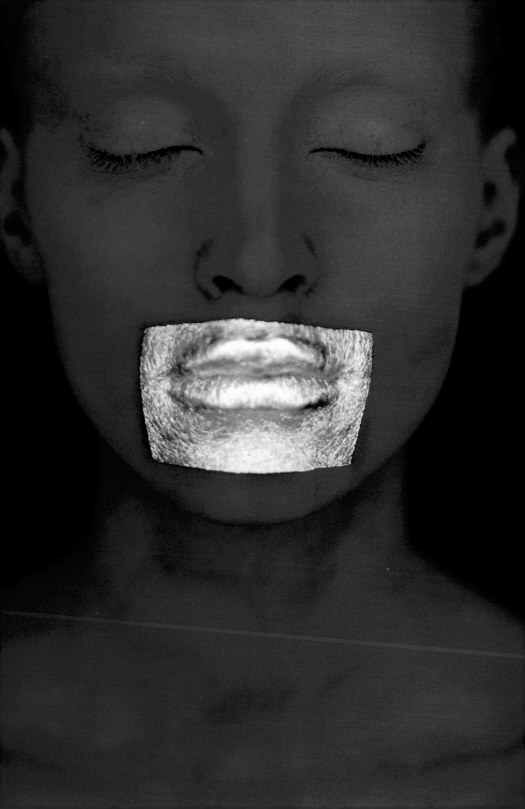

Biography

1965: Topolino was born in Marseilles on January 24th.

1976 : First trip to Paris, which he decides will one day be "his city."

1981 : Leaves school at sixteen and begins work as an apprentice hairstylist.
He takes a correspondence course in fashion styling.
He discovers *Le Palace*.

1982-84: Key encounter with Mr and Mrs Ollier, who hire him for their hairdressing salon (*L'Atelier Parallèle*) where he learns his trade. Topolino tries his hand at everything – beauty care, waxing, manicures, make-up, haircuts, colouring and styling – while continuing his fashion styling course.

1983-84: Topolino creates hair and make-up for short films by young Marseilles film-makers, as well as make-up for theatre productions (Jean Cocteau's *La Belle et la Bête* and *Œdipus*).
He completes his first photo test and fashion shows in southern France.
He decides make-up is his future, and becomes a studio make-up artist.

1984 : Topolino arrives in Paris in May. Luck or destiny, the next day he is hired for his first professional shoot.
He completes numerous tests with young photographers, as hairstylist and make-up artist.
First black-and-white photos for *L'Officiel*.

1985 : He meets Yannick D'Ys with whom he works for over six months.

1986-87: Topolino joins Backstage, a hairstylist/make-up artists agency.
He meets Paolo Roversi, with whom he works.
He works for *20 Ans*, and contributes to first photos by Satoshi ("flower eye"), Ellen Von Unwerth, Denis Chapouillé ("Modigliani") and Stéphane Sednaoui.
First encounter and first photo with Pierre et Gilles.
He begins working with Klaus Wickrath for *Femme*.

1988 : He meets Jean-Baptiste Mondino at the end of the year, leading to their first joint project for *The Face*.
Topolino begins sculpting (which he continues until 1991), showing work at the independent artists' exhibition at the Grand Palais, and in Marseilles (first prize for sculpture).

1989 : Topolino meets Bettina Rheims at the end of her "Modern Lovers" series.
He begins work in London (continuing into the early nineties), where he meets Judy Blame and a generation of young English photographers: Jurgen Teller, Corine Day, David Sims, Marc Le Bon, Eddie Moonson, Glen Luchford, Nina Shultz and Tony Kay.

1990 : Topolino begins working with Bettina on her book, *Les Espionnes*. They still work together today.

1991 : At the end of the year he directs a ten-minute black-and-white film to a Maurice Ravel soundtrack.
Spends one-and-a-half months in Los Angeles with Bettina Rheims, working on a project about Hollywood actresses.

1992 : Topolino, Lionel Bouard and Barnabé set up the Velvet agency. In doing so they offer a creative platform to make-up artists such as Pascale Guichard, Alice Gendhri, Greshka, Fred Farrugia, Dalila, James Kaliardos, and hair-stylists such as Nicolas Jurnjak, Carlos, Clovis and Fouad.

1993 : *Kim*, with Bettina Rheims. Meets Fred Sathal and Philip Treacy.

1994 : Begins work on *Soul* with Thierry Le Goues.

1995 : *Make-up (1985-1995)*, an exhibition of his work at the Marseilles museum of fashion (February to May).

1996 : Velvet closes. Lionel Bouard and Topolino continue their association.
Topolino meets Peter Beard and Helmut Newton, with whom he works.
He receives the 1996 Fashion Award for best make-up artist.

1997 : For six months Topolino works with Bettina Rheims on her book, *INRI*.

2000 : Takes part in the *La Beauté* exhibition and catalogue at Avignon.

2001 : Begins a project on stars which he decides to transform into a personal exhibition.

2002 : Publication of *Make-up Games*.
Stars exhibition at the Marseilles museum of fashion and in Paris.
Plans for a book of Topolino's sketches.

Topolino

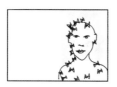

Cat aux papillons (Cat with butterflies).
Paris, 1995.
Photo: Éric Traoré for Pascal Humbert,
fashion show invitation.
Model: Cat.
Hair: Fouad.

Minerve (Minerva).
Paris, 1996.
Photo: Éric Traoré for *Dutch*.
Model: Cat.
Hair: Clovis.
Stylist: Lionel Bouard.

Vénus (Venus).
Paris, 1997.
Photo: Éric Traoré for *Vogue* France.
Model: Inna.
Hair: Clovis.
Stylist: Delphine Tréanton.

Griffes (Claws).
Paris, 1996.
Photo: Éric Traoré for *Dutch*.
Model: Tania Court.
Hair: Clovis.
Stylist: Lionel Bouard.

Bouche bicolore (Two-tone mouth).
Paris, 1996.
Photo: Éric Traoré for *Dutch*.
Model: Cat.
Stylist: Lionel Bouard.

La Mer (The Sea).
Paris, 1998.
Photo: Éric Traoré for *Scène*.
Model: Linda Burns.
Stylist: Lionel Bouard.

Geisha.
Paris, 1998.
Photo: Éric Traoré for *Vogue* France.
Model: Devon Aoki.
Stylist: Delphine Tréanton.

Galaxie (Galaxy).
Paris, 1998.
Photo: Éric Traoré for *Vogue* France.
Model: Linda Burns.
Hair: Clovis.
Stylist: Delphine Tréanton.

Trou noir (Black Hole).
Paris, 2000-2001.
Photo: Alek & Inaki for *Jalouse*.
Model: Olivier Zampol.
Hair: Éric Benazet.
Stylist: Lionel Bouard.

Comète (Comet).
Paris, 2001.
Photo: Alek & Inaki
for the *Les Étoiles* exhibition.
Model: Karine Azur.
Stylist: Lionel Bouard.

Moon Face.
Paris, 2000.
Photo: Les Cyclopes for the
La Beauté exhibition in Avignon.
Model: Sigrid. Hair: Fouad.
Stylist: Lionel Bouard.

Glitter Legs.
Paris, 1998.
Photo: Simon Emmett for *Vogue* France.
Stylist: Marcus.

L'Ouïe (Hearing).
Paris, 1998.
Photo: Éric Traoré for the poster
for the *Les 5 sens* exhibition.
Art director: Philippe Chanet.

Œil graphique (Graphic Eye).
Paris, 1998.
Photo: Éric Traoré for *Vogue* France.
Model: Inna.
Stylist: Delphine Tréanton.

Body Shape.
Paris, 2000-2001.
Photo: Alek & Inaki for *Jalouse*.
Model: Karine Azur.
Stylist: Lionel Bouard.

Car Mask/Ethnic Mask.
New York, 1997.
Photo: Raymond Meier
for the Smart campaign.
Model: Jade.
Hair: Yannick D'Ys.

Gazelle.
Paris, 1998.
Photo: Simon Emmett
for *Vogue* France.
Stylist: Marcus.

1.2.3.
Paris, 2000-2001.
Photo: Alek & Inaki for *Jalouse*.
Model: Sian.
Hair: Éric Benazet.
Stylist: Lionel Bouard.

Sun Marks.
Paris, 1996.
Photo: Jean-Baptiste Mondino for
The Face. Model: Xavier François.
Hair: Odile Gilbert.
Stylist: Friquette.

Ciel étoilé (Starry Sky).
Paris, 2000-2001.
Photo: Alek & Inaki for *Jalouse*.
Model: Olivier Zampol.
Hair: Éric Benazet.
Stylist: Lionel Bouard.

**Kirsten à la marque noire
(Kirsten with a black mark).**
Paris, 1994. Photo: Bettina Rheims for
Détour. Model: Kirsten MacMenamy.
Hair: Renato Campora.
Stylist: Bill Mullen.

Eve.
Paris, 1993.
Photo: Pierre et Gilles.
Model: Michelle Hicks.
Hair: Marc Lopez.
Stylist: Tomah.

Araignée (Spider).
Paris, 1993.
Photo: Mario Testino for *Glamour*.
Model: Olga Patuchenkova.
Hair: Marc Lopez.
Stylist: Carine Roitfeld.

Papillon (Butterfly).
Paris, 1993.
Photo: Mario Testino for *Glamour*.
Model: Olga Patuchenkova.
Hair: Marc Lopez.
Stylist: Carine Roitfeld.

Nina Hagen.
Paris, 1993.
Photo: Pierre et Gilles.
Hair: Marc Lopez.
Stylist: Tomah.

Madame Lola.
Paris, 1996.
Photo: Guido Mocafico for *Citizen K*.
Model: Autruche (Deyrolle).
Stylist: Topolino and Kappauf.

Trendy Cow.
Paris, 1996.
Photo: Guido Mocafico for *Citizen K*.
Model: Super Cow (Deyrolle).
Hair: Topolino.
Stylist: Topolino and Kappauf.

Sainte Lio (Saint Lio).
Paris, 1991.
Photo: Pierre et Gilles for the
Les saintes et les saints exhibition.
Model: Lio.
Stylist: Tomah.

Cover Girl.
Paris, 1997-98.
Photo: Jean-Baptiste Mondino
for *Vogue* France.
Model: Karen Elson.
Hair: Clovis.

Griffes végétales (Plant Claws).
Paris, 1992.
Photo: Norbert Schoerner for *Glamour*.
Model: Mary Cullen.
Stylist: Anne Raybaud.

Œil rond rouge (Red Circle Eye).
New York, 1997.
Photo: Raymond Meier
for the Smart campaign.
Model: Jade.
Hair: Yannick D'Ys.

Œil-fleur (Flower Eye).
Japan, 1987.
Photo: Satoshi Sakusa.
Model: Eugenie Vincent.
Stylist: Mika.

Clown Basic.
Paris, 1993.
Photo: Jean-Baptiste Mondino for
Vogue Homme International.
Model: Nick Moss. Hair: Renato
Campora. Stylist: Melissa Moore.

Clown Bowie.
Paris, 1993.
Photo: Jean-Baptiste Mondino.
Hair: Renato Campora.
Stylist: Melissa Moore.

Red Fontana.
Paris, 1997.
Photo: Éric Traoré for *Vogue* France.
Stylist: Delphine Tréanton.

Shocking Pink.
Paris, 1997-1998.
Photo: Simon Emmett for *Vogue* France.
Model: Clara.
Stylist: Marcus.

Vampire.
Paris, 1999.
Photo: Les Cyclopes, for the
La Beauté exhibition in Avignon.
Model: Rosie. Hair: Fouad.
Stylist: Lionel Bouard.

China Girl.
London, 1997.
Photo: Nick Night for *Visionaire*.
Model: Devon Aoki.
Hair: Clovis. Stylist: Katie England
and Alexander McQueen.

L'étrange Miss (Strange Miss).
London, 1996.
Photo: Phil Poynter for *Dazed
& Confused*. Model: Tanga.
Hair: Barnabé.
Stylist: Katie England.

Sally.
Paris, 2000.
Photo: Les Cyclopes, for the
La Beauté exhibition in Avignon.
Model: Rosie. Hair: Fouad.
Stylist: Lionel Bouard.

Saint Sébastien (Saint Sebastian).
Paris, 1993.
Photo: Jean-Baptiste Mondino
for *The Face*. Model: Charly Degrelle.
Hair: Michael Boadi.
Stylist: Judy Blame.

Urgo.
Paris, 1993.
Photo: Annett Aurel for *ID*.
Model: Karl Pease.
Hair: Barnabé.
Stylist: Annet Monheim.

Christ aux épines (Christ with thorns).
Paris, 1997.
Photo: Bettina Rheims for *INRI*.
Model: Ran.
Hair: Clovis.
Stylist: Suzanne Gunther.

À la Modigliani.
Paris, 1986.
Photo: Denis Chapouillé
for *Jill* and *Photo*. Model: Leslie.
Hair: Barnabé.
Stylist: Fabienne Eisenstein.

Morgue.
Marseilles, 1996.
Photo: Tous des K for the *101 morts*
exhibition. Model: Topolino.
Hair: Topolino.
Stylist: Topolino.

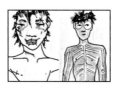

Christ Ecce Homo.
Paris, 1997.
Photo: Bettina Rheims for *INRI*.
Model: Cédric.
Hair: Clovis.
Stylist: Suzanne Gunther.

Pollock.
Paris, 1991.
Photo: Jean-Baptiste Mondino for *ID*.
Model: Zoé Bedot.
Hair: Barnabé.
Stylist: Judy Blame.

Crucifixion.
Photo: Satoshi Sakuza.
Model: Wayne.
Stylist: Mika.

Nu végétal (Plant Nude).
New York, 1994.
Photo: Thierry le Goues for *Soul*.
Hair: Topolino.
Stylist: Topolino.

Foot Hand.
Paris, 1999-2000.
Photo: Les Cyclopes for the
La Beauté exhibition in Avignon.
Art director: Benoît Melleard.

Beauté veinée (Veined Beauty).
New York, 2002.
Photo: Thiemo Sander for *V*.

Audrey en elfe (Audrey as an elf).
Paris, 1998.
Photo: Éric Traoré for *Visionaire*.
Model: Audrey Marnay.
Hair: Clovis.
Art director: Lionel Bouard.

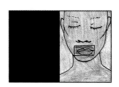

Tribute to Klein.
Paris, 1997.
Photo: Éric Traoré for *Vogue* France.
Model: Inna.
Stylist: Delphine Tréanton.

Bibliography

1990: *Flower Skin*, Claus Wickrath. Cologne, Taschen.

1992: *Les Espionnes*, Bettina Rheims. Munich, Gina Kehayoff.

1994: *Kim*, Bettina Rheims. Munich, Gina Kehayoff.

1995: *Make-up*, Topolino exhibition catalogue. Musée de la Mode de Marseille.
Dictionnaire de la mode du XXᵉ siècle. Paris, Éditions du Regard.

1996: *Fashion, image de la mode*, I. Cologne, Taschen.

1996-97: *Decodex*, Denis Chapouillé. Compagnie DCA.
The Fashion Book. London, Phaidon.

1998: *Fashion, image de la mode*, III. Cologne, Taschen.

1999: *INRI*, Bettina Rheims, Serge Bramly. Paris, Albin Michel.
Déjà vu, Jean-Baptiste Mondino. Munich, Schirmer Mosel.

2000: *Fashion, image de la mode*, IV. Cologne, Taschen.
X'Mas, Bettina Rheims. Paris, Léo Scheer.
La Beauté, exhibition catalogue, Avignon. Paris, Flammarion.
Beauté du siècle, group of authors. Paris, Assouline.

2002: *Morceaux choisis*, Bettina Rheims. Göttingen, Steidl.
Topolino, Make-up Games, group of authors. New York, Assouline.
Les Étoiles, exhibition catalogue. (projet)
Topolino, drawings. (projet)

Contributions:

To exhibitions:
Les Espionnes, Bettina Rheims. Cologne-London, 1992-93.
Make-up, Topolino. Musée de la mode de Marseille, 1995.
Soul, Thierry Le Goues. Paris, Festival de la Mode, 1995.
INRI, Bettina Rheims. Paris-London-Berlin-Prague-Milan..., 1998-1999.
X'Mas, Bettina Rheims. Paris, Galerie Bettina Rheims, 2001.

To videos: Madonna, Neneh Cherry, Jean-Baptiste Mondino, Vanessa Paradis, Lio (with Jean-Pierre Jeunet), Rita Mitsouko, Alain Bashung, MC Solaar.

To album covers: Massive Attack (with Jean-Baptiste Mondino), Björk.

To advertisements: Kodak (with Jean-Baptiste Mondino), Gaultier (with Jean-Baptiste Mondino).

To magazines: *Vogue* (France, Spain, Italy), *Glamour* (France, Italy), *The Face, ID, Dutch, Elle, 20 Ans, L'Officiel, W, Visionaire, V, Citizen K, Jalouse, Femme, Jill*, etc.

To TV programs: Paris Mode (Paris Première), Make-up (Arte), Make-up in Marseilles (FR3), MTV, MCM, Canal+, etc.

To publications: Pierre et Gilles, Peter Beard, Naomi, Visionaire, Helmut Newton, Loana Petrucciani.

Acknowledgments

Topolino wishes to thank: Barnabé, Benoît Melleard and Bertrand, Bettina, Betty Poudre, Blanche-Neige and Maude, Bruce Libre, little Bruno, Catherine and Éric, Charly/Boina and Philippe, Chouchou, Christine Corbel, Dali, Damene, Dinh, D'jani, Fouad, Fred Farrrugia, Golande and Roland, Gonzo and Zorglub, Grégoire the hamster and Ismael, Greshka, Hadji, Iñaki, Jim, Judy Leblame, Kar♥, Kiwi, Lionel, Louise, Magic Magid, Mamie, Marmotte, Maud, Mayia, Michelle and André Ollier, Nadie and Loulou, Nat the Belgian, Nath the painter, Ninon and Aurel, his father and Jo, Peter Beard, Philip Treacy and Stephan, Philippe & Karo & Stéphane, Popeck, Roland, Titou Kutner, Unal la Turquie, Véro.

The models: Audrey Marnay, Cat, Cédric, Charly Degrelle, Clara, Devon Aoki, Eugénie Vincent, Inna, Jade, Karen Elson, Karin Azur, Karl Pease, Kirsten Mac Mennamy, Leslie, Linda Burns, Lio, Lola the ostrich, Mary Cullen, Michelle Hicks, Nick Moss, Nina H., Olga Patuchenckova, Olivier Zampol, Ran, Rosie, Super Cow, Tanga, Tania Court, Wayne, Xavier François, Zazie, Zoe Bedot.

The model agencies: Bananas, City, Fam, Ford, Marilyn, Natalie, Next, Viva.

The hairstylists: Barnabé, Bruce Libre, Clovis, Éric Benazet, Fouad, Marc Lopez, Michael Boadi, Nicolas Jurnjak, Odile Gilbert, Renato Campora, Yannick d'Is.

The photographers: Alec & Iñaki, Annett Aurel, Bettina Rheims, Les Cyclopes, Denis Chapouillé, Éric Traoré, Guido Mocafico, Jean-Baptiste Mondino, Mario Testino, Nick Night, Norbert Schoerner, Phil Poynter, Pierre et Gilles, Raymond Meier, Satoshi, Simon Emmett, Thiemo Sander, Thierry Le Goues, Tous des K.

The stylists and artistic directors: Anne Raybaud, Annet Monheim, Benoît Melleard, Bill Mullen, Carine Roitfeld, Delphine Tréanton, Fabienne Eseinstein, Friquette, Jean Colonna, Judy Blame, Katie England, Lionel Bouard, Melissa Moore, Mika, Philippe Chanet, Suzanne Gunther, Tomah, Topo.

And: Maryline Bellieud Vigouroux, Odette Galeski, Sylvie, Catherine Ormen, Martine, Yaffa and Prosper Assouline, Thomas Cornet, Julie David, the Studio Zéro team, Picto Bastille and the hotel Le Richelieu (Marseilles).

*"1995: Marseilles fashion museum stages
an exhibition of Topolino's work, and the poetic,
lighthearted and original universe of an all-around artist.
We recognize his talent as a leading contemporary artist.
I truly admire his talent and am proud of our friendship."*

Mrs Maryline Bellieud Vigouroux.

All the profits and royalties from this book will be donated to:

ESPACE ARTHUR

Mode Méditerranée

Presided over by Maryline Bellieud Vigouroux

Marseilles, Centre hospitalier de la Thimone

and to ADADI

Directed by Mme Ollier

Espace Arthur is a non-profit body, working with teenagers aged 12 to 18 who are suffering from mental and physical illnesses (anorexia, bulimia, suicide attempts, depression, cancer). It helps them regain their self-confidence, combat their illness and learn to believe in and love themselves.
Adadi is the Beauty-Make-up department of Espace Arthur.